MICROSOFT AZURE

AZ-900

Learn The Basics in One Day

By

Dr Issa Ngoie

What is Cloud Computing?

Cloud = Distance, far

Computing = Operations

Cloud + Computing = Operations
done in
distance

Cloud Services

SAAS: Software as a Service
PAAS: Platform as a Service
IAAS: Infrastruve as a Service

SAAS = Renting of software

PAAS = Renting of a platform
to develop Applications

IAAS = Renting of
Virtual hardware.

Cloud Models

a) <u>Private cloud</u> :- You own
Everything
- You manage
Everything

b) <u>Public cloud</u> :- You own
nothing
- you manage
only your data

Community Cloud :- Belong to
a Community
Such as a church

Note : Public Cloud it a
Shared infrastruve.

Cloud Providers

- Amazon (AWS)
- Microsoft (Azure)
- Google (Google cloud)
- ...

Exercise

1.   What is cloud ?
2.   What is computing
3.   What is cloud computing
4.   List and explain all cloud services.
5.   List and explain all cloud services.
6.   What are the main difference between public and private cloud

Benefits of Cloud Computing

In this module, you'll be introduced to some of the benefits that cloud computing offers. You'll learn how cloud computing can help you meet variable demand while providing a good experience for your customer. You'll also learn about security, governance, and overall manageability in the cloud.

Learning objectives

After reading, you'll be able to:

- ✓ Describe the benefits of high availability and scalability in the cloud.
- ✓ Describe the benefits of reliability and predictability in the cloud.
- ✓ Describe the benefits of security and governance in the cloud.
- ✓ Describe the benefits of manageability in the cloud.

Benefits Of High Availability And Scalability In The Cloud

When building or deploying a cloud application, two of the biggest considerations are uptime (or availability) and the ability to handle demand (or scale).

High availability

When you're deploying an application, a service, or any IT resources, it's important the resources are available when needed. High availability focuses on ensuring maximum availability, regardless of disruptions or events that may occur.

When you're architecting your solution, you'll need to account for service availability guarantees. Azure is a highly available cloud environment with uptime guarantees depending on the service. These guarantees are part of the service-level agreements (SLAs).

Scalability

Another major benefit of cloud computing is the scalability of cloud resources. Scalability refers to the ability to adjust resources to meet demand. If you suddenly experience peak traffic and your systems are overwhelmed, the ability to scale means you can add more resources to better handle the increased demand.

The other benefit of scalability is that you aren't overpaying for services. Because the cloud is a consumption-based model, you only pay for what you use. If demand drops off, you can reduce your resources and thereby reduce your costs.

Scaling generally comes in two varieties: vertical and horizontal. Vertical scaling is focused on increasing or decreasing the capabilities of resources. Horizontal scaling is adding or subtracting the number of resources.

Vertical scaling

With vertical scaling, if you were developing an app and you needed more processing power, you could vertically scale up to add more CPUs or RAM to the virtual machine. Conversely, if you realized you had over-specified the needs, you could vertically scale down by lowering the CPU or RAM specifications.

Horizontal scaling

With horizontal scaling, if you suddenly experienced a steep jump in demand, your deployed resources could be scaled out (either automatically or manually). For example, you could add additional virtual machines or containers, scaling out. In the same manner, if there was a significant drop in demand, deployed resources could be scaled in (either automatically or manually), scaling in.

Exercise

1. What are the benefits of cloud computing?
2. List some disadvantages of cloud computing
3. What is vertical scaling?
4. What is availability?
5. What is scalability?

6. Give an example of a scalable infrastructure

Benefits Of Reliability And Predictability In The Cloud

Reliability and predictability are two crucial cloud benefits that help you develop solutions with confidence.

Reliability

Reliability is the ability of a system to recover from failures and continue to function. It's also one of the pillars of the Microsoft Azure Well-Architected Framework.

The cloud, by virtue of its decentralized design, naturally supports a reliable and resilient infrastructure. With a decentralized design, the cloud enables you to have resources deployed in regions around the world. With this global scale, even if one region has a catastrophic event other regions are still up and running. You can design your applications to automatically take advantage of this increased reliability. In some cases, your cloud environment itself will automatically shift to a different region for you, with no action needed on your part. You'll learn more about how Azure leverages global scale to provide reliability later in this series.

Predictability

Predictability in the cloud lets you move forward with confidence. **Predictability** can be focused on performance predictability or cost predictability. Both performance and cost predictability are heavily influenced by the Microsoft Azure Well-Architected Framework. Deploy a solution that's built around this framework and you have a solution whose cost and performance are predictable.

Performance

Performance predictability focuses on predicting the resources needed to deliver a positive experience for your customers. Autoscaling, load balancing, and high availability are just some of the cloud concepts that support performance predictability. If you suddenly need more resources, autoscaling can deploy additional resources to meet the demand, and then scale back when the demand drops. Or if the traffic is heavily focused on one area, load balancing will help redirect some of the overload to less stressed areas.

Cost

Cost predictability is focused on predicting or forecasting the cost of the cloud spend. With the cloud, you can track your resource use in real time, monitor resources to ensure that you're using them in the most efficient way, and apply data analytics to find patterns and trends that help better plan resource deployments. By operating in the cloud and using cloud analytics and information, you can predict future costs and adjust your resources as needed. You can even use tools like the Total Cost of Ownership (TCO) or Pricing Calculator to get an estimate of potential cloud spend.

Exercise

1. What is availability?
2. What is cost predictability?
3. How azure can set your cost?
4. What is reliability?

Describe the benefits of security and governance in the cloud

Whether you're deploying infrastructure as a service or software as a service, cloud features support governance and compliance. Things like set templates help ensure that all your deployed resources meet corporate standards and government regulatory requirements. Plus, you can update all your deployed resources to new standards as standards change. Cloud-based auditing helps flag any resource that's out of compliance with your corporate standards and provides mitigation strategies. Depending on your operating model, software patches and updates may also automatically be applied, which helps with both governance and security.

On the security side, you can find a cloud solution that matches your security needs. If you want maximum control of security, infrastructure as a service provides you with physical resources but lets you manage the operating systems and installed software, including patches and maintenance. If you want patches and maintenance taken care of automatically, platform as a service or software as a service deployments may be the best cloud strategies for you.

And because the cloud is intended as an over-the-internet delivery of IT resources, cloud providers are typically well suited to handle things like distributed denial of service (DDoS) attacks, making your network more robust and secure.

By establishing a good governance footprint early, you can keep your cloud footprint updated, secure, and well managed.

Exercise

1. Explain how cloud is secured.

2. What is DDoS?
3. What is governance?

Describe the benefits of manageability in the cloud

A major benefit of cloud computing is the manageability options. There are two types of manageability for cloud computing that you'll learn about in this series, and both are excellent benefits.

Management of the cloud

Management of the cloud speaks to managing your cloud resources. In the cloud, you can:

- Automatically scale resource deployment based on need.

- Deploy resources based on a preconfigured template, removing the need for manual configuration.
- Monitor the health of resources and automatically replace failing resources.
- Receive automatic alerts based on configured metrics, so you're aware of performance in real time.

Management in the cloud

Management in the cloud speaks to how you're able to manage your cloud environment and resources. You can manage these:

- ✓ Through a web portal.
- ✓ Using a command line interface.
- ✓ Using APIs.
- ✓ Using PowerShell.

What is Microsoft Azure

Azure is a continually expanding set of cloud services that help you meet current and future business challenges. Azure gives you the freedom to build, manage, and deploy applications on a massive global network using your favorite tools and frameworks.

What does Azure offer?

With help from Azure, you have everything you need to build your next great solution. The following lists several of the benefits that Azure provides, so you can easily invent with purpose:

- **Be ready for the future**: Continuous innovation from Microsoft supports your development today and your product visions for tomorrow.
- **Build on your terms**: You have choices. With a commitment to open source, and support for all languages and frameworks, you can build how you want and deploy where you want.
- **Operate hybrid seamlessly**: On-premises, in the cloud, and at the edge, we'll meet you where you are. Integrate and manage your

environments with tools and services designed
for a hybrid cloud solution.

- **Trust your cloud**: Get security from the
  ground up, backed by a team of experts, and
  proactive compliance trusted by enterprises,
  governments, and startups.

What can I do with Azure?

Azure provides more than 100 services that
enable you to do everything from running
your existing applications on virtual machines
to exploring new software paradigms, such as
intelligent bots and mixed reality.

Many teams start exploring the cloud by
moving their existing applications to virtual
machines (VMs) that run in Azure. Migrating
your existing apps to VMs is a good start, but
the cloud is much more than a different place
to run your VMs.

For example, Azure provides artificial
intelligence (AI) and machine-learning (ML)

services that can naturally communicate with your users through vision, hearing, and speech. It also provides storage solutions that dynamically grow to accommodate massive amounts of data. Azure services enable solutions that aren't feasible without the power of the cloud.

Azure accounts

To create and use Azure services, you need an Azure subscription. When you're completing Learn modules, most of the time a temporary subscription is created for you, which runs in an environment called the Learn sandbox. When you're working with your own applications and business needs, you need to create an Azure account, and a subscription will be created for you. After you've created an Azure account, you're free to create additional subscriptions. For example, your company might use a single Azure account for your business and separate subscriptions for

development, marketing, and sales
departments. After you've created an Azure
subscription, you can start creating Azure
resources within each subscription.

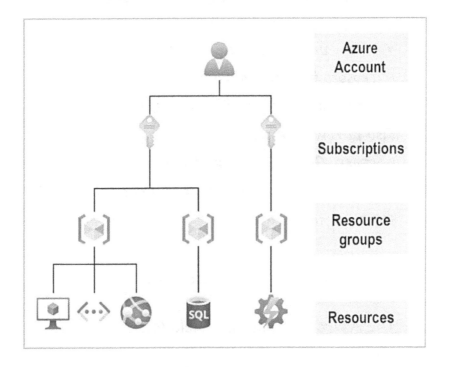

If you're new to Azure, you can sign up for a
free account on the Azure website to start
exploring at no cost to you. When you're
ready, you can choose to upgrade your free
account. You can also create a new
subscription that enables you to start paying

for Azure services you need beyond the limits of a free account.

Create an Azure account

You can purchase Azure access directly from Microsoft by signing up on the Azure website or through a Microsoft representative. You can also purchase Azure access through a Microsoft partner. Cloud Solution Provider partners offer a range of complete managed-cloud solutions for Azure.

What is the Azure free account?

The Azure free account includes:

- Free access to popular Azure products for 12 months.
- A credit to use for the first 30 days.
- Access to more than 25 products that are always free.

The Azure free account is an excellent way for new users to get started and explore. To sign up, you need a phone number, a credit card, and a Microsoft or GitHub account. The credit card information is used for identity verification only. You won't be charged for any services until you upgrade to a paid subscription.

What is the Azure free student account?

The Azure free student account offer includes:

- Free access to certain Azure services for 12 months.
- A credit to use in the first 12 months.
- Free access to certain software developer tools.

The Azure free student account is an offer for students that gives $100 credit and free developer tools. Also, you can sign up without a credit card.

What is the Microsoft Learn sandbox?

Many of the Learn exercises use a technology called the sandbox, which creates a temporary subscription that's added to your Azure account. This temporary subscription allows you to create Azure resources during a Learn module. Learn automatically cleans up the temporary resources for you after you've completed the module.

When you're completing, you're welcome to use your personal subscription to complete the exercises in a module. However, the sandbox is the preferred method to use because it allows you to create and test Azure resources at no cost to you.

Exercise

1. What is azure account?
2. How to open an azure account?
3. What is Microsoft azure?

4. What is azure subscription?

Azure physical infrastructure

Throughout your journey with Microsoft Azure, you'll hear and use terms like Regions, Availability Zones, Resources, Subscriptions, and more. This module focuses on the core architectural components of Azure. The core architectural components of Azure may be broken down into two main groupings: the physical infrastructure, and the management infrastructure.

Physical infrastructure

The physical infrastructure for Azure starts with datacenters. Conceptually, the datacenters are the same as large corporate datacenters. They're facilities with resources arranged in racks, with dedicated power, cooling, and networking infrastructure.

As a global cloud provider, Azure has datacenters around the world. However, these individual datacenters aren't directly accessible. Datacenters are grouped into Azure Regions or Azure Availability Zones that are designed to help you achieve resiliency and reliability for your business-critical workloads.

The Global infrastructure site gives you a chance to interactively explore the underlying Azure infrastructure.

Regions

A region is a geographical area on the planet that contains at least one, but potentially multiple datacenters that are nearby and networked together with a low-latency network. Azure intelligently assigns and controls the resources within each region to ensure workloads are appropriately balanced.

When you deploy a resource in Azure, you'll often need to choose the region where you want your resource deployed.

Note

Some services or virtual machine (VM) features are only available in certain regions, such as specific VM sizes or storage types. There are also some global Azure services that don't require you to select a particular region, such as Microsoft Entra ID, Azure Traffic Manager, and Azure DNS.

Availability Zones

Availability zones are physically separate datacenters within an Azure region. Each availability zone is made up of one or more datacenters equipped with independent power, cooling, and networking. An availability zone is set up to be an isolation boundary. If one zone

goes down, the other continues working.
Availability zones are connected through high-speed, private fiber-optic networks.

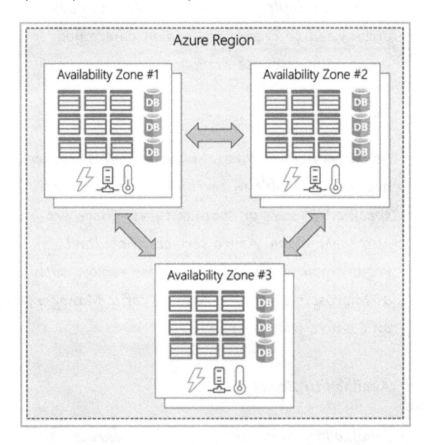

Important

To ensure resiliency, a minimum of three
separate availability zones are present in all
availability zone-enabled regions. However, not

all Azure Regions currently support availability zones.

Use availability zones in your apps

You want to ensure your services and data are redundant so you can protect your information in case of failure. When you host your infrastructure, setting up your own redundancy requires that you create duplicate hardware environments. Azure can help make your app highly available through availability zones.

You can use availability zones to run mission-critical applications and build high-availability into your application architecture by co-locating your compute, storage, networking, and data resources within an availability zone and replicating in other availability zones. Keep in mind that there could be a cost to duplicating your services and transferring data between availability zones.

Availability zones are primarily for VMs, managed disks, load balancers, and SQL databases. Azure services that support availability zones fall into three categories:

- **Zonal services**: You pin the resource to a specific zone (for example, VMs, managed disks, IP addresses).
- **Zone-redundant services**: The platform replicates automatically across zones (for example, zone-redundant storage, SQL Database).
- **Non-regional services**: Services are always available from Azure geographies and are resilient to zone-wide outages as well as region-wide outages.

Even with the additional resiliency that availability zones provide, it's possible that an event could be so large that it impacts multiple availability zones in a single region. To provide even further resilience, Azure has Region Pairs.

Region pairs

Most Azure regions are paired with another region within the same geography (such as US, Europe, or Asia) at least 300 miles away. This approach allows for the replication of resources across a geography that helps reduce the likelihood of interruptions because of events such as natural disasters, civil unrest, power outages, or physical network outages that affect an entire region. For example, if a region in a pair was affected by a natural disaster, services would automatically fail over to the other region in its region pair.

Important

Not all Azure services automatically replicate data or automatically fall back from a failed region to cross-replicate to another enabled region. In these scenarios, recovery and replication must be configured by the customer.

Examples of region pairs in Azure are West US paired with East US and South-East Asia paired with East Asia. Because the pair of regions are directly connected and far enough apart to be isolated from regional disasters, you can use them to provide reliable services and data redundancy.

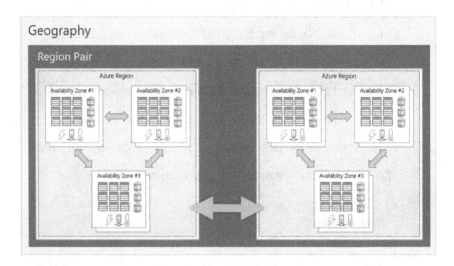

Additional advantages of region pairs:

- If an extensive Azure outage occurs, one region out of every pair is prioritized to make sure at least one is restored as quickly as possible for applications hosted in that region pair.

- Planned Azure updates are rolled out to paired regions one region at a time to minimize downtime and risk of application outage.
- Data continues to reside within the same geography as its pair (except for Brazil South) for tax- and law-enforcement jurisdiction purposes.

Important

Most regions are paired in two directions, meaning they are the backup for the region that provides a backup for them (West US and East US back each other up). However, some regions, such as West India and Brazil South, are paired in only one direction. In a one-direction pairing, the Primary region does not provide backup for its secondary region. So, even though West India's secondary region is South India, South India does not rely on West India. West India's secondary region is South India, but South India's secondary region is Central India. Brazil South is unique because it's paired with a region outside of its geography. Brazil South's secondary region is South Central US. The secondary region of South Central US isn't Brazil South.

Sovereign Regions

In addition to regular regions, Azure also has sovereign regions. Sovereign regions are instances of Azure that are isolated from the main instance of Azure. You may need to use a sovereign region for compliance or legal purposes.

Azure sovereign regions include:

- US DoD Central, US Gov Virginia, US Gov Iowa and more: These regions are physical and logical network-isolated instances of Azure for U.S. government agencies and partners. These datacenters are operated by screened U.S. personnel and include additional compliance certifications.
- China East, China North, and more: These regions are available through a unique partnership between Microsoft and 21Vianet,

whereby Microsoft doesn't directly maintain the datacenters.

Exercise

1. What is azure region?
2. What is azure availability zone?
3. What is a zone?
4. What is a datacenter?
5. What is a virtual machine?

Microsoft Azure Fundamentals: Describe Azure management and governance

Cost Management In Azure

In this chapter , you'll be introduced to factors that impact costs in Azure and tools to help you both predict potential costs and monitor and control costs.

Learning objectives

After reading, you'll be able to:

- Describe factors that can affect costs in Azure.
- Compare the Pricing calculator and Total Cost of Ownership (TCO) calculator.
- Describe the Microsoft Cost Management Tool.
- Describe the purpose of tags.

Factors That Can Affect Costs In Azure

The following video provides an introduction to things that can impact your costs in Azure.

Azure shifts development costs from the capital expense (CapEx) of building out and maintaining infrastructure and facilities to an operational expense (OpEx) of renting infrastructure as you need it, whether it's compute, storage, networking, and so on.

That OpEx cost can be impacted by many factors. Some of the impacting factors are:

✓ Resource type
✓ Consumption
✓ Maintenance
✓ Geography
✓ Subscription type
✓ Azure Marketplace

Resource type

A number of factors influence the cost of Azure resources. The type of resources, the settings for the resource, and the Azure region will all have an impact on how much a resource costs. When you provision an Azure resource, Azure creates metered instances for that resource. The meters track the resources' usage and generate a usage record that is used to calculate your bill.

Examples

With a storage account, you specify a type such as blob, a performance tier, an access tier, redundancy settings, and a region. Creating the same storage account in different regions may show different costs and changing any of the settings may also impact the price.

Blob storage

Enable SFTP ⓘ	☐
	ⓘ To enable SFTP, 'hierarchical namespace' must be enabled.
Enable network file system v3 ⓘ	☐
	ⓘ To enable NFS v3 'hierarchical namespace' must be enabled. Learn more about NFS v3
Allow cross-tenant replication ⓘ	☑
Access tier ⓘ	⦿ **Hot:** Frequently accessed data and day-to-day usage scenarios
	○ **Cool:** Infrequently accessed data and backup scenarios

With a virtual machine (VM), you may have to consider licensing for the operating system or other software, the processor and number of cores for the VM, the attached storage, and the network interface. Just like with storage, provisioning the same virtual machine in different regions may result in different costs.

Create a virtual machine

Basics   Disks   Networking   Management   Advanced   Tags   Review + create

Create a virtual machine that runs Linux or Windows. Select an image from Azure marketplace or use your own customized image. Complete the Basics tab then Review + create to provision a virtual machine with default parameters or review each tab for full customization. Learn more ⌕

Project details

Select the subscription to manage deployed resources and costs. Use resource groups like folders to organize and manage all your resources.

Subscription * ⓘ | Visual Studio Enterprise Subscription   ⌄ |

      Resource group * ⓘ | (New) Resource group   ⌄ |
                           Create new

Instance details

Virtual machine name * ⓘ | |

Region * ⓘ   Your recently used sizes

Availability options ⓘ   Standard_D2s_v3 - 2 vcpus, 8 GiB memory

Security type ⓘ   Recommended by image publisher

Image * ⓘ   Standard_DS1_v2 - 1 vcpu, 3.5 GiB memory

                                Standard_D4s_v3 - 4 vcpus, 16 GiB memory

                                Standard_E2s_v3 - 2 vcpus, 16 GiB memory

Azure Spot instance ⓘ   See all sizes

Size * ⓘ | Standard_D2s_v3 - 2 vcpus, 8 GiB memory   ⌄ |

Consumption

Pay-as-you-go has been a consistent theme throughout, and that's the cloud payment model where you pay for the resources that you use during a billing cycle. If you use more compute this cycle, you pay more. If you use less in the current cycle, you pay less. It's a straight forward pricing mechanism that allows for maximum flexibility.

However, Azure also offers the ability to commit to using a set amount of cloud resources in advance and receiving discounts on those "reserved" resources. Many services, including databases, compute, and storage all provide the option to commit to a level of use and receive a discount, in some cases up to 72 percent.

When you reserve capacity, you're committing to using and paying for a certain amount of Azure resources during a given period (typically one or three years). With the back-up of pay-as-you-go, if you see a sudden surge in demand that eclipses what you've pre-reserved, you just pay for the additional resources in excess of your reservation. This model allows you to recognize significant savings on reliable, consistent workloads while also having the flexibility to rapidly increase your cloud footprint as the need arises.

Maintenance

The flexibility of the cloud makes it possible to rapidly adjust resources based on demand. Using resource groups can help keep all of your resources organized. In order to control costs, it's important to maintain your cloud environment. For example, every time you provision a VM, additional resources such as storage and networking are also provisioned. If you deprovision the VM, those additional resources may not deprovision at the same time, either intentionally or unintentionally. By keeping an eye on your resources and making sure you're not keeping around resources that are no longer needed, you can help control cloud costs.

Geography

When you provision most resources in Azure, you need to define a region where the resource deploys. Azure infrastructure is distributed globally, which enables you to deploy your services centrally or closest to your customers, or something in between. With this global deployment comes global pricing differences. The cost of power, labor, taxes, and fees vary depending on the location. Due to these variations, Azure resources can differ in costs to deploy depending on the region.

Network traffic is also impacted based on geography. For example, it's less expensive to move information within Europe than to move information from Europe to Asia or South America.

Network Traffic

Billing zones are a factor in determining the cost of some Azure services.

Bandwidth refers to data moving in and out of Azure datacenters. Some inbound data transfers (data going into Azure datacenters) are free. For outbound data transfers (data leaving Azure datacenters), data transfer pricing is based on zones.

A zone is a geographical grouping of Azure regions for billing purposes. The <u>bandwidth pricing page</u> has additional information on pricing for data ingress, egress, and transfer.

Subscription type

Some Azure subscription types also include usage allowances, which affect costs.

For example, an Azure free trial subscription provides access to a number of Azure products that are free for 12 months. It also includes credit to spend within your first 30 days of sign-up. You'll get access to more than 25 products that are always free (based on resource and region availability).

Azure Marketplace

Azure Marketplace lets you purchase Azure-based solutions and services from third-party vendors. This could be a server with software preinstalled and configured, or managed network firewall appliances, or connectors to third-party backup services. When you purchase products through Azure Marketplace, you may pay for not only the Azure services that you're using, but also the services or expertise of the third-party vendor. Billing structures are set by the vendor.

All solutions available in Azure Marketplace are certified and compliant with Azure policies and standards. The certification policies may vary based on the service or solution type and Azure service involved. _Commercial marketplace certification policies_ has additional information on Azure Marketplace certifications.

Compare the Pricing and Total Cost of Ownership calculators

The pricing calculator and the total cost of ownership (TCO) calculator are two calculators that help you understand potential Azure expenses. Both calculators are accessible from the internet, and both calculators allow you to build out a configuration. However, the two calculators have very different purposes.

Pricing calculator

The pricing calculator is designed to give you an estimated cost for provisioning resources in Azure. You can get an estimate for individual resources, build out a solution, or use an example scenario to see an estimate of the

Azure spend. The pricing calculator's focus is on the cost of provisioned resources in Azure.

 Note

The Pricing calculator is for information purposes only. The prices are only an estimate. Nothing is provisioned when you add resources to the pricing calculator, and you won't be charged for any services you select.

With the pricing calculator, you can estimate the cost of any provisioned resources, including compute, storage, and associated network costs. You can even account for different storage options like storage type, access tier, and redundancy.

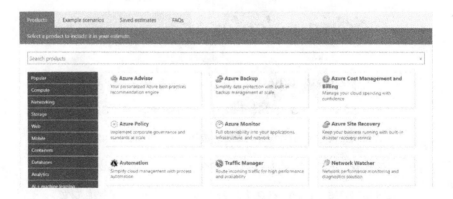

Microsoft Azure

TCO calculator

The TCO calculator is designed to help you compare the costs for running an on-premises infrastructure compared to an Azure Cloud infrastructure. With the TCO calculator, you enter your current infrastructure configuration, including servers, databases, storage, and outbound network traffic. The TCO calculator then compares the anticipated costs for your current environment with an Azure environment supporting the same infrastructure requirements.

With the **TCO calculator**, you enter your configuration, add in assumptions like power and IT labor costs, and are presented with an estimation of the cost difference to run the same environment in your current datacenter or in Azure.

Azure terms

Azure Cosmos DB

A great solution when your architecture requires solutions other than relational databases. It's a multi-model, globally distributed database service from Microsoft that provides high availability and minimal latency. It is a fully flexible and scalable solution that is a good choice if you operate on large datasets and you want to make them available to users in a very short time.

Azure Cache (Redis)

The cache of the Azure platform, which is based on Redis software. The caching data solution significantly increases the efficiency and scalability of the application. Using Redis in the cloud provides much greater benefits because it creates and manages many Redis nodes. Data in the cache is protected additionally, so you do not have to be worried about data security aspects

Azure SQL Database

A cloud-based relational MS SQL database that is shared as a managed service. Using the SQL Server in the cloud relieves you of many administrative tasks, such as periodic backups and updates. Such a database easily communicates with services dispersed in the cloud or on different servers.

Azure Storage

Scalable cloud storage on the Azure platform. It's a very good solution when you need space to store different types of data, such as graphic files, documents, binary messages, etc. Different types of storage allow you to select the one that optimally meets your needs.

Azure Service Bus

The perfect queuing tool to ensure reliable asynchronous communication between your services. It's perfect for <u>microservices architecture.</u>

Serverless (Azure Functions)

A <u>serverless</u> solution that allows you to create applications even faster and simpler. You can use one of the many programming languages available to implement the service. An additional advantage of this solution is the ability to fully integrate with the cloud environment, based on the events of your application. Depending on the selected variant, you will pay only for the time when your service is really active (pay-per-use pricing model).

www.ingramcontent.com/pod-product-compliance
Lightning Source LLC
Chambersburg PA
CBHW060443060326
40690CB00019B/4317

* 9 7 9 8 8 7 1 9 4 5 2 7 8 *